BALTIMORE CATECHISM ONE

Also known as

A CATECHISM *of* CHRISTIAN DOCTRINE NO. 1

Imprimatur: ✠ John Cardinal McCloskey
Archbishop of New York
New York, April 6, 1885

"The Catechism ordered by The Third Plenary Council of Baltimore, having been diligently compiled and examined, is hereby approved."

✠ James Gibbons
Archbishop of Baltimore
Apostolic Delegate
Baltimore, April 6, 1885

Imprimatur for Word Meanings:

Nihil obstat: ✠ Remy Lafort
Censor Librorum
New York, July 25, 1898

Imprimatur: ✠ Michael Augustine
Archbishop of New York
New York, July 25, 1898

Nihil obstat: ✠ Arthur J. Scanlan, S.T.D.
Censor Librorum
New York, November 26, 1932

Imprimatur: Patrick Cardinal Hayes
Archbishop of New York
New York, November 26, 1932

BALTIMORE CATECHISM ONE

Prepared and Enjoined by Order of The Third Plenary Council of Baltimore

WITH PHONETICIZED WORDS, AND WORD MEANINGS

QUESTIONS NUMBERED TO AGREE WITH "EXPLANATION OF THE BALTIMORE CATECHISM"

With Prayers and Hymns

TAN·CLASSICS

TAN Books, a division of Saint Benedict Press, LLC.

Originally issued by the Third Plenary Council of Baltimore in 1885. This edition reprinted from the 1933 edition of Benziger Brothers, Inc. by arrangement with Benziger, Bruce and Glencoe, Inc.

Published with the assistance of The Livingstone Corporation. Cover and interior design by Mark Wainright, The Livingstone Corporation. Typeset by TAN Books.

Cover Image: *The wise men's offering to the infant saviour* by English School (20th century) Private Collection/Look and Learn/The Bridgeman Art Library.

ISBN: 978-0-89555-144-3

Printed and bound in India

13 12 11 10 9 8 7 6 5 4

www.TANBooks.com

TAN·CLASSICS

CONTENTS

PRAYERS

The Lord's Prayer

Our Father, Who art in Heaven, hallowed be Thy name; Thy kingdom come; Thy will be done on earth as it is in Heaven. Give us this day our daily bread; and forgive us our trespasses as we forgive those who trespass against us: and lead us not into temptation, but deliver us from evil. Amen.

The Angelical Salutation

Hail Mary, full of grace! The Lord is with thee: blessed art thou amongst women, and blessed is the fruit of thy womb, Jesus. Holy Mary, Mother of God, pray for us sinners, now and at the hour of our death. Amen.

The Apostles' Creed

I believe in God, the Father Almighty, Creator of Heaven and earth; and in Jesus Christ, His only Son, Our Lord; who was conceived by the Holy Ghost, born of the Virgin Mary, suffered under Pontius Pilate, was crucified; died, and was buried. He descended into Hell; the third day He arose again from the dead; He ascended into Heaven, sitteth at the right hand of God, the Father Almighty; from thence He shall come to judge the living and the dead.

I believe in the Holy Ghost, the Holy Catholic Church, the communion of Saints, the forgiveness of sins, the resurrection of the body, and the life everlasting. Amen.

The Confiteor

I confess to Almighty God, to Blessed Mary, ever Virgin, to Blessed Michael the Archangel, to Blessed John the Baptist, to the Holy Apostles Peter and Paul, and to all the Saints, that I have sinned exceedingly in thought, word and deed, through my fault, through my fault, through my most grievous fault. Therefore, I beseech Blessed Mary, ever Virgin, Blessed Michael the Archangel, Blessed John the Baptist, the Holy Apostles Peter and Paul, and all the Saints, to pray to the Lord our God for me.

May the Almighty God have mercy on me, and forgive me my sins, and bring me to everlasting life. Amen.

May the Almighty and merciful Lord grant me pardon, absolution and remission of all my sins. Amen.

An Act of Faith

O my God! I firmly believe that Thou art one God in three Divine Persons, Father, Son, and Holy Ghost; I believe that Thy Divine Son became man, and died for our sins, and that He will come to judge the living and the dead. I believe these and all the truths which the Holy Catholic Church teaches, because Thou hast revealed them, who canst neither deceive nor be deceived.

An Act of Hope

O my God! Relying on Thy infinite goodness and promises, I hope to obtain pardon of my sins, the help of Thy grace, and life everlasting, through the merits of Jesus Christ, my Lord and Redeemer.

An Act of Love

O my God! I love Thee above all things, with my whole heart and soul, because Thou art all-good and worthy of all love. I love my neighbor as myself for the love of Thee. I forgive all who have injured me, and ask pardon of all whom I have injured.

An Act of Contrition

O my God! I am heartily sorry for having offended Thee, and I detest all my sins, because I dread the loss of Heaven and the pains of Hell, but most of all because they offend Thee, my God, who art all-good and deserving of all my love. I firmly resolve, with the help of Thy grace, to confess my sins, to do penance, and to amend my life.

The Blessing before Meals

✠ Bless us, O Lord! and these Thy gifts, which we are about to receive from Thy bounty, through Christ Our Lord. Amen.

Grace after Meals

✠ We give Thee thanks for all Thy benefits, O Almighty God, who livest and reignest forever; and may the souls of the faithful departed through the mercy of God, rest in peace. Amen.

The Manner in Which a Lay Person Is to Baptize in Case of Necessity

Pour common water on the head or face of the person to be baptized, and say while pouring it:

"I baptize thee in the name of the Father, and of the Son, and of the Holy Ghost."

N.B. Any person of either sex who has reached the use of reason can baptize in case of necessity, but the same person must say the words while pouring the water.

CATECHISM

KEY TO PRONUNCIATION

ā as in face
â as in chocolate
â as in dare
ă as in act
ä as in farm
ȧ as in tall
ē as in eve

ĕ as in edge
ẽ as in baker
ī as in like
ĭ as in fin
ō as in old
ô as in or
ŏ as in oft

ū as in huge
ŭ as in up
û as in burn
o͞o as in mood
o͝o as in brook
ou as in out

LESSON FIRST

On the End of Man

A-pos′tles (ȧ-pŏs′′lz), the twelve men chosen by Christ to carry on His work.

Chief (chēf), the most important.

Com-posed′ (kŏm-pōzd′), made up of.

Cre-a′tor (krē-ā′tẽr), the One who made all things out of nothing.

Crea′ture (krē′tūr), everything made by God out of nothing.

Creed (krēd), a list of the principal truths of faith in a few words.

End, the purpose for which we are made.

Serve (sẽrv), to do His holy will.

Soul (sōl), the spirit in man giving life to the body.

Wor′ship (wûr′shĭp), to pay God the honor due Him alone, to adore.

1. Q. Who made the world?

A. God made the world.

2. Q. Who is God?

A. God is the Creator of Heaven and earth, and of all things.

3. Q. What is man?

A. Man is a creature composed of body and soul, and made to the image and likeness of God.

6. Q. Why did God make you?

A. God made me to know Him, to love Him, and to serve Him in this world, and to be happy with Him forever in Heaven.

9. Q. What must we do to save our souls?

A. To save our souls we must worship God by faith, hope, and charity; that is, we must believe in Him, hope in Him, and love Him with all our heart.

10. Q. How shall we know the things which we are to believe?

A. We shall know the things which we are to believe from the Catholic Church, through which God speaks to us.

11. Q. Where shall we find the chief truths which the Church teaches?

A. We shall find the chief truths which the Church teaches in the Apostles' Creed.

12. Say the Apostles' Creed.

LESSON SECOND

On God and His Perfections

Im-pos′si-ble (ĭm-pŏs′ĭ-b'l), can not be done.

In′fi-nite′ly (ĭn′fĭ-nĭt′lĭ), beyond measure.

Mer′ci-ful (mûr′sĭ-fŭl), kind, and forgiving.

Per′fect (pĕr′fĕkt), so good that nothing can be better.

Per-fec′tions (pĕr-fĕk′shŭnz), good qualities.

Se′cret (sē′krĕt), known only to myself.

13. Q. What is God?

A. God is a spirit infinitely perfect.

14. Q. Had God a beginning?

A. God had no beginning; He always was and He always will be.

15. Q. Where is God?

A. God is everywhere.

16. Q. If God is everywhere, why do we not see Him?

A. We do not see God, because He is a pure spirit and cannot be seen with bodily eyes.

17. Q. Does God see us?

A. God sees us and watches over us.

18. Q. Does God know all things?

A. God knows all things, even our most secret thoughts, words, and actions.

19. Q. Can God do all things?

A. God can do all things, and nothing is hard or impossible to Him.

20. Q. Is God just, holy, and merciful?

A. God is all just, all holy, all merciful, as He is infinitely perfect.

LESSON THIRD

On the Unity and Trinity of God

Dis-tinct′ (dĭs-tĭnkt′), separate, different.

Di-vine′ Na′ture (dĭ-vīn′ nā′tūr), that which is one in God.

E′qual (ē′kwăl), another just as great and perfect as Himself.

In′fi-nite (ĭn′fĭ-nĭt), the most perfect possible.

Su-preme′ (sū-prēm′), above all.

Trin′i-ty (trĭn′ĭ-tĭ), three in one.

U′ni-ty (ū′nĭ-tĭ), being only one.

21. Q. Is there but one God?

A. Yes; there is but one God.

22. Q. Why can there be but one God?

A. There can be but one God, because God, being supreme and infinite, cannot have an equal.

23. Q. How many Persons are there in God?

A. In God there are three Divine Persons, really distinct, and equal in all things—the Father, the Son, and the Holy Ghost.

24. Q. Is the Father God?

A. The Father is God and the first Person of the Blessed Trinity.

25. Q. Is the Son God?

A. The Son is God and the second Person of the Blessed Trinity.

26. Q. Is the Holy Ghost God?

A. The Holy Ghost is God and the third Person of the Blessed Trinity.

27. Q. What is the Blessed Trinity?

A. The Blessed Trinity is one God in three Divine Persons.

28. Q. Are the three Divine Persons one and the same God?

A. The three Divine Persons are one and the same God, having one and the same Divine Nature.

LESSON FOURTH

On The Angels and Our First Parents

A-dore′ (ȧ-dōr′), to worship, to honor in the highest degree.

Be-fell′ (bē-fĕl′), happened to.

Bod′i-less (bŏd′ĭ-lĕs), having no body.

Com-mand′ (kŏ-mȧnd′), an order.

Con-cep′tion (kŏn-sĕp′shŭn), joining of soul and body at the beginning of life.

Cre-at′ed (krē-āt′ĕd), made, as God alone can make, out of nothing.

Dis′o-be′di-ence (dĭs′ō-bē′dĭ-ĕns), refusing to obey.

Doomed (do͞omd), condemned.

E′vil (ē′v'l), harm; that which causes unhappiness.

Faith′ful (fāth′fŭl), true, steady in obedience.

For-bid′den (fôr-bĭd′ĕn), that which we are told not to do.

Guilt (gĭlt), stain, taint.

Im-mac′u-late (ĭ-măk′ū-lȃt), not stained by sin of any kind.

In-her′it (ĭn-hĕr′ĭt), to come into possession of through our parents or by will.

In′no-cent (ĭn′ō-sĕnt), free from all sin.

Mer′its (mĕr′ĭts), what Jesus won by the Redemption.

O-rig′i-nal (ō-rĭj′ĭ-năl), the first, from which the others flow.

Pre-served′ (prē-zûrvd′), kept free from, excepted from.

Priv′i-lege (prĭv′ĭ-lĕj), exceptional favor.

Pun′ish-ment (pŭn′ĭsh-mĕnt), suffering sent on them.

Shared (shârd), had a part in.

34. Q. Which are the chief creatures of God?

A. The chief creatures of God are men and angels.

35. Q. What are angels?

A. Angels are bodiless spirits created to adore and enjoy God in Heaven.

39. Q. Who were the first man and woman?

A. The first man and woman were Adam and Eve.

40. Q. Were Adam and Eve innocent and holy when they came from the hand of God?

A. Adam and Eve were innocent and holy when they came from the hand of God.

43. Q. Did Adam and Eve remain faithful to God?

A. Adam and Eve did not remain faithful to God; but broke His command by eating the forbidden fruit.

44. Q. What befell Adam and Eve on account of their sin?

A. Adam and Eve on account of their sin lost innocence and holiness, and were doomed to misery and death.

45. Q. What evil befell us through the disobedience of our first parents?

A. Through the disobedience of our first parents we all inherit their sin and punishment, as we should have shared in their happiness if they had remained faithful.

47. Q. What is the sin called which we inherit from our first parents?

A. The sin which we inherit from our first parents is called Original Sin.

50. Q. Was any one ever preserved from Original Sin?

A. The Blessed Virgin Mary, through the merits of her Divine Son, was preserved free from the guilt of Original Sin, and this privilege is called her Immaculate Conception.

LESSON FIFTH

On Sin and Its Kinds

Ac′tu-al (ăk′tū-ăl) sin, the sin which we, ourselves, commit.

Cap′i-tal (kăp′ĭ-tăl), the heads, the sources of others.

Com-mit′ (kŏ-mĭt′), to do, to be guilty of.

Com′mon-ly (kŏm′ŭn-lĭ), usually.

Con-sent′ (kŏn-sĕnt′), giving in to.

Con′tra-ry (kŏn′trȧ-rĭ), against.

Cov′et-ous-ness (kŭv′ĕ-tŭs-nĕs), too great a desire for money or goods.

Deed (dēd), an act.

En′vy (ĕn′vĭ), sadness at another's welfare.

Glut′ton-y (glŭt′′nĭ), eating or drinking too much.

Griev′ous (grēv′ŭs), very great.

Im-por′tance (ĭm-pôr′tăns), of account.

Lust (lŭst), strong desire for impure thoughts, words or actions.

Mat′ters (măt′ĕrz), the acts done.

Mor′tal (môr′tăl), that which kills the soul; deadly.

Of-fense′ (ŏ-fĕns′), fault.

O-mis′sion (ō-mĭsh′ŭn), a duty left undone.

Pride (prīd), taking credit to ourselves for what was given us by God.

Re-flec′tion (rē-flĕk′-shŭn), thinking a thing over.

Sloth (slŏth), laziness which keeps us from doing our duty.

Suf-fi′cient (sŭ-fĭsh′ĕnt), enough to know whether it is right or wrong.

Ve′ni-al (vē′nĭ-ăl), that which is more easily forgiven.

Will′ful (wĭl′fŭl), done on purpose.

51. Q. Is Original Sin the only kind of sin?

A. Original Sin is not the only kind of sin; there is another kind of sin, which we commit ourselves, called actual sin.

52. Q. What is actual sin?

A. Actual sin is any willful thought, word, deed or omission contrary to the law of God.

53. Q. How many kinds of actual sin are there?

A. There are two kinds of actual sin—mortal and venial.

54. Q. What is mortal sin?

A. Mortal sin is a grievous offense against the law of God.

57. Q. What is venial sin?

A. Venial sin is a slight offense against the law of God in matters of less importance; or in matters of great importance it is an offense committed without sufficient reflection or full consent of the will.

59. Q. Which are the chief sources of sin?

A. The chief sources of sin are seven: Pride, Covetousness, Lust, Anger, Gluttony, Envy, and Sloth; and they are commonly called capital sins.

LESSON SIXTH

On the Incarnation and Redemption

A-ban′don (ȧ-băn′dŭn), to leave one helpless.

An-nounced′ (ă-nounst′), made known.

An-nun′ci-a′tion (ă-nŭn′-sē-ā′-shŭn), the making known, announcing—March 25.

Beth′le-hem (bĕth′lĕ-hĕm), a small town in the Holy Land.

Christ, the Anointed.

Con-ceived′ (kŏn-sēvd′), given life to.

In′car-na′tion (ĭn′kär-nā′shŭn), the act of becoming man.

Je′sus, Saviour, Deliverer.

Man′kind (măn′kīnd), all the people of the world.

Re-deem′er (rē-dēm′ẽr), the One who was to deliver man from the slavery of sin.

Re-demp′tion (rē-dĕmp′-shŭn), the deliverance from sin and its punishment by the death of Christ.

Re-o′pen (rē-ō′p'n), to open again.

Sat′is-fy (săt′ĭs-fī), pay in full for.

60. Q. Did God abandon man after he fell into sin?

A. God did not abandon man after he fell into sin, but promised him a Redeemer, who was to satisfy for man's sin and reopen to him the gates of Heaven.

61. Q. Who is the Redeemer?

A. Our Blessed Lord and Saviour Jesus Christ is the Redeemer of mankind.

62. Q. What do you believe of Jesus Christ?

A. I believe that Jesus Christ is the Son of God, the second Person of the Blessed Trinity, true God and true man.

69. Q. What do you mean by the Incarnation?

A. By the Incarnation I mean that the Son of God was made man.

70. Q. How was the Son of God made man?

A. The Son of God was conceived and made man by the power of the Holy Ghost, in the womb of the Blessed Virgin Mary.

74. Q. On what day was the Son of God conceived and made man?

A. The Son of God was conceived and made man on Annunciation day—the day on which the angel Gabriel announced to the Blessed Virgin Mary that she was to be the Mother of God.

75. Q. On what day was Christ born?

A. Christ was born on Christmas day in a stable at Bethlehem, over nineteen hundred years ago.

LESSON SEVENTH

On Our Lord's Passion, Death, Resurrection, and Ascension

As-cend′ed (ă-sĕnd′ĕd), went up.

As-cen′sion (ă-sĕn′shŭn), the act of going up into Heaven.

Cru′ci-fied (krū′sĭ-fīd), nailed hands and feet to a cross.

Glo′ri-ous (glō′rĭ-ŭs), bright, shining.

Im-mor′tal (ĭ-môr′tăl), never to die.

Pas′sion (păsh′ŭn), the last great sufferings of our Saviour.

Res′ur-rec′tion (rĕz′ŭ-rĕk′shŭn), the rising again from the dead.

Scourg′ing (skûrj′ĭng), lashing with a whip.

78. Q. What did Jesus Christ Suffer?

A. Jesus Christ suffered a bloody sweat, a cruel scourging, was crowned with thorns, and was crucified.

79. Q. On what day did Christ die?

A. Christ died on Good Friday.

83. Q. Why did Christ suffer and die?

A. Christ suffered and died for our sins.

89. Q. On what day did Christ rise from the dead?

A. Christ rose from the dead, glorious and immortal, on Easter Sunday, the third day after His death.

91. Q. After Christ had remained forty days on earth, whither did He go?

A. After forty days Christ ascended into Heaven, and the day on which He ascended into Heaven is called Ascension day.

LESSON EIGHTH

On the Holy Ghost and His Descent upon the Apostles

De-scent′ (dē-sĕnt′), the act of coming down.
En-a′ble (ĕn-ā′b'l), to make able.
En-light′en (ĕn-līt′′n), to make them understand better.
Pen′te-cost (pĕn′tĕ-kŏst), the fiftieth day after Easter.
Preach (prēch), declare publicly, spread by word of mouth.
Sanc′ti-fy (sănk′tĭ-fī), to make holy.
Strength′en (strĕng′th'n), make strong.
Whit′sun-day (hwĭt′s'n-dā), white Sunday.

94. Q. Who is the Holy Ghost?
A. The Holy Ghost is the third Person of the Blessed Trinity.

97. Q. On what day did the Holy Ghost come down upon the Apostles?
A. The Holy Ghost came down upon the Apostles ten days after the Ascension of Our Lord; and the day on which He came down upon the Apostles is called Whitsunday, or Pentecost.

99. Q. Who sent the Holy Ghost upon the Apostles?
A. Our Lord Jesus Christ sent the Holy Ghost upon the Apostles.

100. Q. Why did Christ send the Holy Ghost?

A. Christ sent the Holy Ghost to sanctify His Church, to enlighten and strengthen the Apostles, and to enable them to preach the Gospel.

LESSON NINTH

On the Effects of the Redemption

Be-stowed′ (bē-stōd′), given as a favor.

Ef-fects′ (ĕ-fĕkts′), results, consequences.

E-ter′nal (ē-tẽr′năl) **life**, the never-ending happiness of Heaven.

Jus′tice (jŭs′tĭs), justness.

Mer′its (mĕr′ĭts), the rewards earned by His sufferings and death.

Neigh′bor (nā′bẽr), everyone in the world.

Ob-tain′ (ŏb-tān′), to get.

Re-vealed′ (rē-vēld′), made known by God.

Sal-va′tion (săl-vā′shŭn), the saving of our soul.

Sat′is-fac′tion (săt′ĭs-făk′shŭn), making payment, in some way, to God for what we owe Him by our sins.

Shun (shŭn), to keep clear of, avoid.

Su′per-nat′u-ral (sū′pẽr-năt′ū-răl), above nature.

Trust (trŭst), to look for confidently.

Vir′tue (vûr′tū), the habit of doing good.

102. Q. Which are the chief effects of the Redemption?

A. The chief effects of the Redemption are two: The satisfaction of God's justice by Christ's sufferings and death, and the gaining of grace for men.

103. Q. What do you mean by grace?

A. By grace I mean a supernatural gift of God bestowed on us, through the merits of Jesus Christ, for our salvation.

104. Q. How many kinds of grace are there?

A. There are two kinds of grace: sanctifying grace and actual grace.

105. Q. What is sanctifying grace?

A. Sanctifying grace is that grace which makes the soul holy and pleasing to God.

110. Q. What is actual grace?

A. Actual grace is that help of God which enlightens our mind and moves our will to shun evil and do good.

107. Q. What is Faith?

A. Faith is a Divine virtue by which we firmly believe the truths which God has revealed.

108. Q. What is Hope?

A. Hope is a Divine virtue by which we firmly trust that God will give us eternal life and the means to obtain it.

109. Q. What is Charity?

A. Charity is a Divine virtue by which we love God above all things for His own sake, and our neighbor as ourselves for the love of God.

LESSON TENTH

On the Church

Ap´os-tol´ic (ăp´ŏs-tŏl´-ĭk), coming down from the Apostles.
Bish´op (bĭsh´ŏp), head of a diocese.
Cath´o-lic (kăth´ō-lĭk), spread all over the world, universal.
Con´gre-ga´tion (kŏn´grĕ-gā´-shŭn), a union of people, a society.
Fruits (frūts), benefits, results.
Gov´erned (gŭv´ĕrnd), ruled.
In´sti-tut´ed (ĭn´stĭ-tūt´-ĕd), given or appointed.
In-vis´i-ble (ĭn-vĭz´ĭ-b'l), that which cannot be seen.
Law´ful (lô´fŭl), by right, according to the Church's laws.
Marks, distinctive signs.
Means (mēnz), aids, helps.
One, united in government and teaching.
Par-take´ (pär-tāk´) **of**, to receive, share in.
Pope (pōp), the father of the faithful, head of the Church.
Pro-fess´ (prō-fĕs´), to let it be known publicly.
Ro´man (rō´măn), so called because the See of St. Peter is in Rome.
Sac´ra-ments (săk´rȧ-mĕnts), outward signs of grace.
Vic´ar (vĭk´ĕr), a person acting in the name and with the authority of another.
Vis´i-ble (vĭz´ĭ-b'l), that which can be seen.

114. Q. Which are the means instituted by Our Lord to enable men at all times to share in the fruits of the Redemption?

A. The means instituted by Our Lord to enable men at all times to share in the fruits of His Redemption are the Church and the Sacraments.

115. Q. What is the Church?

A. The Church is the congregation of all those who profess the faith of Christ, partake of the same Sacraments, and are governed by their lawful pastors under one visible Head.

116. Q. Who is the invisible Head of the Church?

A. Jesus Christ is the invisible Head of the Church.

117. Q. Who is the visible Head of the Church?

A. Our Holy Father the Pope, the Bishop of Rome, is the Vicar of Christ on earth, and the visible Head of the Church.

128. Q. Has the Church any marks by which it may be known?

A. The Church has four marks by which it may be known: it is One; it is Holy; it is Catholic; it is Apostolic.

133. Q. In which Church are these marks found?

A. These marks are found in the Holy Roman Catholic Church alone.

LESSON ELEVENTH

On the Sacraments in General

Bap´tism (băp´tĭzm), a washing.

Con´fir-ma´tion (kŏn´fẽr-mā´-shŭn), the strengthening of our faith.

Dis´po-si´tions (dĭs´pō-zĭsh´ŭnz), state of mind and heart.

Eu´cha-rist (ū´kȧ-rĭst), a giving of thanks.

Ex-treme´ (ĕks-trēm´), the last.

Holy Orders, holy ranks, the sacred ministry.

In gen´er-al, taken together.

Mat´ri-mo-ny (măt´rĭ-mō-nĭ), marriage.

Out´ward (out´wẽrd), that which can be seen, heard or felt.

Pen´ance (pĕn´ăns), sorrow for offending God.

Sign, that which stands for something else.

Unc´tion (ŭnk´shŭn), the anointing or rubbing with oil.

136. Q. What is a Sacrament?

A. A Sacrament is an outward sign instituted by Christ to give grace.

137. Q. How many Sacraments are there?

A. There are seven Sacraments: Baptism, Confirmation, Holy Eucharist, Penance, Extreme Unction, Holy Orders, and Matrimony.

138. Q. Whence have the Sacraments the power of giving grace?

A. The Sacraments have the power of giving grace from the merits of Jesus Christ.

147. Q. Do the Sacraments always give grace?

A. The Sacraments always give grace, if we receive them with the right dispositions.

148. Q. Can we receive the Sacraments more than once?

A. We can receive the Sacraments more than once, except Baptism, Confirmation, and Holy Orders.

LESSON TWELFTH

On Baptism

Ad-min′is-ter (ăd-mĭn′ĭs-tẽr), give or perform.
Chris′tians (krĭs′chănz), members of the Church of Christ.
Cleans′es (klĕnz′ĕz), washes, frees.
Guil′ty (gĭl′tĭ), have committed.
Heirs (ârz), inheritors, entitled to.
Min′is-ter (mĭn′ĭs-tẽr), one who performs any of the sacred rites or ceremonies of the Church.
Nec′es-sa-ry (nĕs′ĕ-sā-rĭ), what one cannot do without.
Ne-ces′si-ty (nĕ-sĕs′ĭ-tĭ), when Baptism must be given [on account of danger of death] and a priest cannot be had.
Or′di-na-ry (ôr′dĭ-nā-rĭ), usual or regular.
Re-mit′ted (rē-mĭt′ĕd), blotted out.
Rightly dis-posed′ (dĭs-pōzd′), heartily sorry for his sins.
Use of reason, sense to know right from wrong.

152. Q. What is Baptism?

A. Baptism is a Sacrament which cleanses us from Original Sin, makes us Christians, children of God, and heirs of Heaven.

153. Q. Are actual sins ever remitted by Baptism?

A. Actual sins and all the punishment due to them are remitted by Baptism, if the person baptized be guilty of any, and is rightly disposed.

154. Q. Is Baptism necessary to salvation?

A. Baptism is necessary to salvation, because without it we cannot enter into the kingdom of Heaven.

155. Q. Who can administer Baptism?

A. The priest is the ordinary minister of Baptism; but in case of necessity anyone who has the use of reason may baptize.

156. Q. How is Baptism given?

A. Whoever baptizes should pour water on the head of the person to be baptized, and say, while pouring the water: *I baptize thee in the name of the Father, and of the Son, and of the Holy Ghost.*

LESSON THIRTEENTH

On Confirmation

A-noints′ (ȧ-noints′), rubs with oil.
Chrism (krĭs'm), a mixture of olive oil and balm, consecrated by the Bishop.
Es-pe′cial-ly (ĕs-pĕsh′ăl-lĭ), principally, above all.
E′vil (ē′v'l), wicked.
Ex-posed′ (ĕks-pōzd′), laid open, subject to.
Ex-tends′ (ĕks-tĕndz′), spreads out.
Form (fôrm), shape.
Mor′als (môr′ălz), good conduct.
Per′fect (pēr′fĕkt), very good.
Temp-ta′tions (tĕmp-tā′shŭnz), whatever might draw one into sin.
Vi′o-lent (vī′ō-lĕnt), very strong.
Wor′thi-ly (wûr′thĭ-lĭ), in the right way.

166. Q. What is Confirmation?

A. Confirmation is a Sacrament through which we receive the Holy Ghost to make us strong and perfect Christians and soldiers of Jesus Christ.

167. Q. Who administers Confirmation?

A. The Bishop is the ordinary minister of Confirmation.

168. Q. How does the Bishop give Confirmation?

A. The Bishop extends his hands over those who are to be confirmed, prays that they may receive the Holy Ghost, and anoints the forehead of each with holy chrism in the form of a cross.

170. Q. What does the Bishop say in anointing the person he confirms?

A. In anointing the person he confirms the Bishop says: *I sign thee with the Sign of the Cross, and I confirm thee with the chrism of salvation, in the name of the Father, and the Son, and of the Holy Ghost.*

173. Q. To receive Confirmation worthily is it necessary to be in the state of grace?

A. To receive Confirmation worthily it is necessary to be in the state of grace.

174. Q. What is a state of grace?

A. A state of grace is freedom from mortal sin.

175. Q. Is it a sin to neglect Confirmation?

A. It is a sin to neglect Confirmation, especially in these evil days when faith and morals are exposed to so many and such violent temptations.

LESSON FOURTEENTH

On the Sacrament of Penance

Ac-cept′ the pen′ance, consent to do what the priest tells us to do for our sins.

Com-mit′ted (kŏ-mĭt′ĕd), done.

Con-fess′ (kŏn-fĕs′), to tell.

Con′science (kŏn′shĕns), that within us which tells us when we do wrong.

Ear′nest (ûr′nĕst) **ef′fort**, doing our very best.

Ex-am′ine (ĕg-zăm′ĭn), to ask questions of ourselves.

Firm (fûrm), strong.

Res′o-lu′tion (rĕz′ō-lū′shŭn), making up our mind.

Wor′thy (wûr′thĭ), good.

187. Q. What is the Sacrament of Penance?

A. Penance is a Sacrament in which the sins committed after Baptism are forgiven.

191. Q. What must we do to receive the Sacrament of Penance worthily?

A. To receive the Sacrament of Penance worthily we must do five things:

1. We must examine our conscience.
2. We must have sorrow for our sins.
3. We must make a firm resolution never more to offend God.
4. We must confess our sins to the priest.
5. We must accept the penance which the priest gives us.

192. Q. What is the examination of conscience?

A. The examination of conscience is an earnest effort to recall to mind all the sins we have committed since our last worthy Confession.

LESSON FIFTEENTH

On Contrition

A-void′ (ȧ-void′), keep away from.

Con-demns′ (kŏn-dĕmz′), sentences.

E′vils (ē′v′lz), things which do harm to us.

Fixed re-solve′ (rē-zŏlv′), deciding once for all.

Ha′tred (hā′trĕd), strong dislike.

Of-fense′ (ŏ-fĕns′), sin, crime, insult.

Of-fend′ed (ŏ-fĕnd′ĕd), displeased.

Pre-serv′er (prē-zûrv′ĕr), the One who keeps us alive.

Pur′pose (pûr′pŭs), resolution, intention.

195. Q. What is contrition, or sorrow for sin?

A. Contrition, or sorrow for sin, is a hatred of sin, and a true grief of the soul for having offended God, with a firm purpose of sinning no more.

201. Q. Why should we be sorry for our sins?

A. We should be sorry for our sins, because sin is the greatest of evils and an offense against God our Creator, Preserver, and Redeemer, and because mortal sin shuts us out of Heaven and condemns us to the eternal pains of Hell.

206. Q. What do you mean by a firm purpose of sinning no more?

A. By a firm purpose of sinning no more I mean a fixed resolve not only to avoid all mortal sin, but also its near occasions.

207. Q. What do you mean by the near occasions of sin?

A. By the near occasions of sin I mean all the persons, places, and things that may easily lead us into sin.

LESSON SIXTEENTH

On Confession

Con-ceal′ (kŏn-sēl′), to hide or keep back.
Du′ly au′thor-ized (dū′lī ŏ′-thŏr-īzd), appointed by the Bishop.
For the purpose, with the intention.
Ob-tain′ing (ŏb-tān′ĭng), receiving.
Re-peat′ (rē-pēt′), say over again; tell once more to the confessor.
Tem′po-ral (tĕm′pō-răl), lasting for a time only.
There-by′ (thâr-bī′), by so doing.
Will′ful-ly (wĭl′fŭl-ĭ), on purpose.
Worth′less (wûrth′lĕs), no good at all.

208. Q. What is Confession?

A. Confession is the telling of our sins to a duly authorized priest, for the purpose of obtaining forgiveness.

209. Q. What sins are we bound to confess?

A. We are bound to confess all our mortal sins, but it is well also to confess our venial sins.

214. Q. What should we do if we cannot remember the number of our sins?

A. If we cannot remember the number of our sins, we should tell the number as nearly as possible.

216. Q. Is it a grievous offense willfully to conceal a mortal sin in Confession?

A. It is a grievous offense willfully to conceal a mortal sin in Confession, because we thereby tell a lie to the Holy Ghost and make our Confession worthless.

217. Q. What must he do who has willfully concealed a mortal sin in Confession?

A. He who has willfully concealed a mortal sin in Confession must not only confess it, but must also repeat all the sins he has committed since his last worthy Confession.

218. Q. Why does the priest give us a penance after Confession?

A. The priest gives us a penance after Confession that we may satisfy God for the temporal punishment due to our sins.

LESSON SEVENTEENTH

On Indulgences

Due (dū), owed.
En-joined′ (ĕn-joind′), ordered to be done.
Full, complete.
In whole, altogether, entirely.
Par′tial (pär′shăl), in part only.
Per-form′ (pĕr-fôrm′), do.
Ple′na-ry (plē′nȧ-rĭ), full, complete.
Re-mis′sion (rē-mĭsh′ŭn), taking away.
State of grace, free from mortal sin.

231. Q. What is an Indulgence?
A. An Indulgence is the remission in whole or in part of the temporal punishment due to sin.

233. Q. How many kinds of Indulgences are there?
A. There are two kinds of Indulgences—Plenary and Partial.

234. Q. What is a Plenary Indulgence?
A. A Plenary Indulgence is the full remission of the temporal punishment due to sin.

235. Q. What is a Partial Indulgence?
A. A Partial Indulgence is the remission of a part of the temporal punishment due to sin.

237. Q. What must we do to gain an Indulgence?
A. To gain an Indulgence we must be in the state of grace and perform the works enjoined.

LESSON EIGHTEENTH

On the Holy Eucharist

Com-mem′o-ra′tion (kŏ-mĕm′ō-rā′shŭn), a calling to mind.

Con′se-cra′tion (kŏn′sĕ-krā′-shŭn), the act of changing the bread and wine into the sacred Body and Blood of Christ.

Di-vin′i-ty (dĭ-vĭn′ĭ-tĭ), the nature of God.

Ex′er-cise (ĕk′sĕr-sīz), make use of.

Sens′es (sĕns′ĕz), the sight, the taste, the touch, etc.

238. Q. What is the Holy Eucharist?

A. The Holy Eucharist is the Sacrament which contains the Body and Blood, Soul and Divinity, of Our Lord Jesus Christ under the appearances of bread and wine.

245. Q. What do you mean by the appearances of bread and wine?

A. By the appearances of bread and wine I mean the figure, the color, the taste, and whatever appears to the senses.

249. Q. When did Christ give His priests the power to change bread and wine into His Body and Blood?

A. Christ gave His priests the power to change bread and wine into His Body and Blood when He said to the Apostles, "Do this for a commemoration of Me."

250. Q. How do the priests exercise this power of changing bread and wine into the Body and Blood of Christ?

A. The priests exercise this power of changing bread and wine into the Body and Blood of Christ through the words of Consecration in the Mass, which are the words of Christ: "This is My body; this is My blood."

LESSON NINETEENTH

On the Ends for Which the Holy Eucharist Was Instituted

Con-tin′ue (kŏn-tĭn′ū), keep on repeating a thing.
In′cli-na′tions (ĭn′klĭ-nā′shŭnz), strong likings.
In-crease′ (ĭn-krēs′), to make greater.
In′sti-tut-ed (ĭn′stĭ-tūt-ĕd), begun, established.
Nour′ish (nŭr′ĭsh), to support with food.
Pledge (plĕj), promise.
Sac′ri-fice (săk′rĭ-fīs), an offering made to God.
Sac′ri-lege (săk′rĭ-lĕj), showing disrespect for a holy thing.
Sanc′ti-fy-ing (sănk′tĭ-fī-ĭng), making holy.
U-nite′ (ū-nīt′), join.
Vir′tues (vûr′tūz), habits of doing good.

251. Q. Why did Christ institute the Holy Eucharist?

A. Christ instituted the Holy Eucharist:

1. To unite us to Himself and to nourish our soul with His Body and Blood.
2. To increase sanctifying grace and all virtues in our soul.
3. To lessen our evil inclinations.
4. To be a pledge of everlasting life.
5. To fit our bodies for a glorious resurrection.
6. To continue the Sacrifice of the Cross in His Church.

253. Q. What is Holy Communion?

A. Holy Communion is the receiving of the Body and Blood of Christ.

254. Q. What is necessary to make a good Communion?

A. To make a good Communion it is necessary to be in the state of grace and to be fasting for one hour from food and all drinks, except water.[1]

255. Q. Does he who receives Communion in mortal sin receive the Body and Blood of Christ?

A. He who receives Communion in mortal sin receives the Body and Blood of Christ, but does not receive His grace, and he commits a great sacrilege.

1. This answer has been changed in the 1977 edition to bring it up to date with the current rules.

LESSON TWENTIETH

On the Sacrifice of the Mass

As-sist′ (ă-sĭst′), to be present at.

De-vo′tion (dē-vō′shŭn), earnestness, strong love for God.

In-te′ri-or (ĭn-tē′rĭ-ĕr), in our heart.

Pi′e-ty (pī′ĕ-tĭ), holy thoughts or affection for God.

Rec′ol-lec′tion (rĕk′ō-lĕk′shŭn), remembering where we are and what we are doing.

Re-spect′ (rē-spĕkt′), esteem, regard, reverence.

262. Q. When are the bread and wine changed into the Body and Blood of Christ?

A. The bread and wine are changed into the Body and Blood of Christ at the Consecration in the Mass.

263. Q. What is the Mass?

A. The Mass is the unbloody Sacrifice of the Body and Blood of Christ.

265. Q. Is the Mass the same Sacrifice as that of the Cross?

A. The Mass is the same Sacrifice as that of the Cross.

269. Q. How should we assist at Mass?

A. We should assist at Mass with great interior recollection and piety, and with every outward mark of respect and devotion.

LESSON TWENTY-FIRST

On Extreme Unction and Holy Orders

Com′fort (kŭm′fẽrt), to refresh, to encourage.
Ef-fects′ (ĕ-fĕkts′), results.
Ex-treme′ (ĕks-trēm′), the very last.
Min′is-ters (mĭn′ĭs-tẽrz), deacons and sub-deacons.
Or-dained′ (ôr-dānd′), set apart for a certain office, appointed.
Re-mains′ (rē-mānz′) **of sin**, the bad habits caused by sin.
Re-store′ (rē-stôr′), to bring back.
Sa′cred (sā′krĕd), holy.
Temp-ta′tions (tĕm-tā′shŭnz), that which draws us to sin.
Unc′tion (ŭnk′shŭn), rubbing with oil.

271. Q. What is the Sacrament of Extreme Unction?

A. Extreme Unction is the Sacrament which, through the anointing and prayer of the priest, gives health and strength to the soul, and sometimes to the body, when we are in danger of death from sickness.

274. Q. Which are the effects of the Sacrament of Extreme Unction?

A. The effects of Extreme Unction are: 1) to comfort us in the pains of sickness and to strengthen us against temptations; 2) to remit venial sins and to cleanse our soul from the remains of sin; 3) to restore us to health, when God sees fit.

276. Q. What is the Sacrament of Holy Orders?

A. Holy Orders is a Sacrament by which bishops, priests, and other ministers of the Church are ordained and receive the power and grace to perform their sacred duties.

LESSON TWENTY-SECOND

On Matrimony

Com-ply′ (kŏm-plī′) **with**, to act according to.
Law′ful (lô′fŭl), according to law.
Sanc′ti-fy (sănk′tĭ-fĭ), make holy.
Weak′nes-ses (wēk′nĕs-ĕz), faults and failings.

282. Q. What is the Sacrament of Matrimony?

A. The Sacrament of Matrimony is the Sacrament which unites a Christian man and woman in lawful marriage.

285. Q. Which are the effects of the Sacrament of Matrimony?

A. The effects of the Sacrament of Matrimony are: 1) to sanctify the love of husband and wife; 2) to give them grace to bear with each other's weaknesses; 3) to enable them to bring up their children in the fear and love of God.

286. Q. To receive the Sacrament of Matrimony worthily is it necessary to be in the state of grace?

A. To receive the Sacrament of Matrimony worthily it is necessary to be in the state of grace, and it is necessary also to comply with the laws of the Church.

LESSON TWENTY-THIRD

On the Sacramentals

Cru´ci-fix-es (krū´sĭ-fĭk-sĕz), crosses with a figure of Our Lord on them.

Ex-cite´ (ĕk-sīt´), to stir up.

Fre´quent (frē´kwĕnt), happening often.

Im´a-ges (ĭm´ȧ-jĕz), statues, pictures, etc.

In-crease´ (ĭn-krēs´), to make greater.

Mys´ter-ies (mĭs´tĕr-ĭz), truths that we cannot understand, but which are made known to us by God.

Palms (päms), branches of the palm tree.

Powers of darkness, the devil and his bad angels.

Pro-fess´ (prō-fĕs´), to let people see.

Pro-tec´tion (prō-tĕk´shŭn), help.

Re-mit´ (rē-mĭt´), to forgive.

Ro´sa-ries (rō´zȧ-rĭz), prayer-beads.

Sac´ra-men´tals (săk´rȧ-mĕn´-tălz), something blessed or set apart by the Church.

Scap´u-lars (skăp´ū-lȧrz), two pieces of cloth joined by strings and worn over the shoulders.

Sol´emn (sŏl´ĕm), with special ceremonies.

292. Q. What is a sacramental?

A. A sacramental is anything set apart or blessed by the Church to excite good thoughts and to increase devotion, and through these movements of the heart to remit venial sin.

294. Q. Which is the chief sacramental used in the Church?

A. The chief sacramental used in the Church is the Sign of the Cross.

295. Q. How do we make the Sign of the Cross?

A. We make the Sign of the Cross by putting the right hand to the forehead, then on the breast, and then to the left and right shoulders, saying, "In the name of the Father, and of the Son, and of the Holy Ghost. Amen."

296. Q. Why do we make the Sign of the Cross?

A. We make the Sign of the Cross to show that we are Christians and to profess our belief in the chief mysteries of our religion.

300. Q. What other sacramental is in very frequent use?

A. Another sacramental in very frequent use is holy water.

301. Q. What is holy water?

A. Holy water is water blessed by the priest with solemn prayer to beg God's blessing on those who use it, and protection from the powers of darkness.

302. Q. Are there other sacramentals besides the Sign of the Cross and holy water?

A. Besides the Sign of the Cross and holy water there are many other sacramentals, such as blessed candles, ashes, palms, crucifixes, images of the Blessed Virgin and of the Saints, rosaries and scapulars.

LESSON TWENTY-FOURTH

On Prayer

Af-flic′tions (ă-flĭk′shŭnz), sufferings in mind or body.
A-vail′ (ȧ-vāl′), profit or advantage.
Con-fi′te-or (kŏn-fē′tā-ōr), I confess.
Dis-trac′tions (dĭs-trăk′shŭnz), thinking of other things besides your prayers.
Means (mēnz), that by help of which we gain something.
Ob-tain′ing (ŏb-tān′ĭng), getting.
Par-tic′u-lar (pär-tĭk′ū-lȧr), special.
Rec′om-mend′ed (rĕk′ŏ-mĕnd′ĕd), praised.

303. Q. Is there any other means of obtaining God's grace than the Sacraments?
A. There is another means of obtaining God's grace, and it is prayer.

304. Q. What is prayer?
A. Prayer is the lifting up of our minds and hearts to God to adore Him, to thank Him for His benefits, to ask His forgiveness, and to beg of Him all the graces we need, whether for soul or body.

305. Q. Is prayer necessary to salvation?
A. Prayer is necessary to salvation, and without it no one having the use of reason can be saved.

306. Q. At what particular times should we pray?

A. We should pray particularly on Sundays and Holy Days, every morning and night, in all dangers, temptations, and afflictions.

308. Q. Which are the prayers most recommended to us?

A. The prayers most recommended to us are the *Lord's Prayer*, the *Hail Mary*, the *Apostles' Creed*, the *Confiteor*, and the *Acts of Faith, Hope, Love* and *Contrition*.

309. Q. Are prayers said with distractions of any avail?

A. Prayers said with willful distractions are of no avail.

LESSON TWENTY-FIFTH

On the Commandments of God

A-dul′ter-y (ȧ-dŭl′tĕr-ĭ), the sin of impurity.

Bear false witness, to tell lies about.

Com-mand′ments (kŏ-mȧnd′-mĕnts), laws.

Cov′et (kŭv′ĕt), to be greedy for, to desire.

Goods, riches, or whatever he owns.

Hon′or (ŏn′ĕr), respect and obey.

In vain, take, utter, invoke without necessity or in fun.

Neigh′bor (nā′bĕr), everyone in the world.

Sab′bath (săb′ȧth) **day**, the Lord's day, now Sunday.

Strange (strānj), false.

310. Q. Is it enough to belong to God's Church in order to be saved?

A. It is not enough to belong to the Church in order to be saved, but we must also keep the Commandments of God and of the Church.

313. Q. Which are the Commandments of God?

A. The Commandments of God are these ten:

1. I am the Lord thy God. Thou shalt not have strange gods before Me.
2. Thou shalt not take the name of the Lord thy God in vain.
3. Remember thou keep holy the Sabbath day.
4. Honor thy father and thy mother.
5. Thou shalt not kill.

6. Thou shalt not commit adultery.
7. Thou shalt not steal.
8. Thou shalt not bear false witness against thy neighbor.
9. Thou shalt not covet thy neighbor's wife.
10. Thou shalt not covet thy neighbor's goods.

LESSON TWENTY-SIXTH

On the First Commandment

A-dore′ (ȧ-dōr′), to give God the honor due Him alone.

At-trib′ut-ing (ȧ-trĭb′ū-tĭng), referring.

Bro′ken, disobeyed.

Ex′pec-ta′tion (ĕks′pĕk-tā′shŭn), a looking forward to.

False wor′ship (wûr′shĭp) worshipping God not as He directs, but in a way pleasing to ourselves.

Open pro-fes′sion (prō-fĕsh′ŭn), a public declaration.

Pre-sump′tion (prē-zŭmp′shŭn), taking for granted the saving of one's soul.

Rash (răsh), foolish.

Spir′it-u-al (spĭr′ĭt-ū-ăl) **good**, the good of one's soul.

315. Q. What is the first Commandment?

A. The first Commandment is: "I am the Lord thy God: thou shalt not have strange gods before Me."

317. Q. How do we adore God?

A. We adore God by faith, hope, and love, by prayer and sacrifice.

318. Q. How may the first Commandment be broken?

A. The first Commandment may be broken by giving to a creature the honor which belongs to God alone; by false worship; and by attributing to a creature a perfection which belongs to God alone.

320. Q. Are sins against faith, hope, and charity also sins against the first Commandment?

A. Sins against faith, hope, and charity are also sins against the first Commandment.

321. Q. How does a person sin against faith?

A. A person sins against faith, 1) by not trying to know what God has taught; 2) by refusing to believe all that God has taught; 3) by neglecting to profess his belief in what God has taught.

326. Q. Are we obliged to make open profession of our faith?

A. We are obliged to make open profession of our faith as often as God's honor, our neighbor's spiritual good, or our own requires it.

327. Q. Which are the sins against hope?

A. The sins against hope are presumption and despair.

328. Q. What is presumption?

A. Presumption is a rash expectation of salvation without making proper use of the necessary means to obtain it.

329. Q. What is despair?

A. Despair is the loss of hope in God's mercy.

LESSON TWENTY-SEVENTH

The First Commandment—On the Honor and Invocation of Saints

Af-fec′tions (ă-fĕk′shŭnz), feelings.
Ap-proves′ (ă-pro͞ovz′), is in accord with.
Di-rect′ly con-nect′ed (dĭ-rĕkt′lĭ kō-nĕkt′ĕd), closely joined.
En-liv′en (ĕn-līv′ĕn), to stir up.
Ex-cit′ing (ĕk-sīt′ĭng), causing.
Im′i-tate (ĭm′ĭ-tāt), to copy.
Me-mo′ri-als (mĕ-mō′rĭ-ălz), something to remind us.
Rel′ics (rĕl′ĭks), bones of the Saints or objects connected with them or Our Lord.
Rep′re-sen-ta′tions (rĕp′rĕ-zĕn-tā′shŭnz), means of showing the appearance of absent ones.

331. Q. Does the first Commandment forbid the honoring of the Saints?

A. The first Commandment does not forbid the honoring of the Saints, but rather approves of it, because by honoring the Saints, who are the chosen friends of God, we honor God Himself.

332. Q. Does the first Commandment forbid us to pray to the Saints?

A. The first Commandment does not forbid us to pray to the Saints.

333. Q. What do we mean by praying to the Saints?

A. By praying to the Saints we mean the asking of their help and prayers.

340. Q. Does the first Commandment forbid us to honor relics?

A. The first Commandment does not forbid us to honor relics, because relics are the bodies of the Saints or objects directly connected with them or with Our Lord.

341. Q. Does the first Commandment forbid the making of images?

A. The first Commandment does forbid the making of images if they are made to be adored as gods, but it does not forbid the making of them to put us in mind of Jesus Christ, His Blessed Mother, and the Saints.

342. Q. Is it right to show respect to the pictures and images of Christ and His Saints?

A. It is right to show respect to the pictures and images of Christ and His Saints, because they are the representations and memorials of them.

343. Q. Is it allowed to pray to the crucifix or to the images and relics of the Saints?

A. It is not allowed to pray to the crucifix or images and relics of the Saints, for they have no life, nor power to help us, nor sense to hear us.

344. Q. Why do we pray before the crucifix and the images and relics of the Saints?

A. We pray before the crucifix and the images and relics of the Saints because they enliven our devotion by exciting pious affections and desires, and by reminding us of Christ and of the Saints, that we may imitate their virtues.

LESSON TWENTY-EIGHTH

From the Second to the Fourth Commandment

Blas′phem-y (blȧs′fĕ-mĭ), saying or doing something disrespectful to God or holy things.

Curs′ing (kûrs′ĭng), calling upon God to bring evils on another.

De-lib′er-ate (dē-lĭb′ĕr-ât), well considered beforehand.

Due (dū), right and proper.

Ful-fill′ (fŭl-fĭl′), to carry out, to do as promised.

Hin′der (hĭn′dĕr), prevent.

Ho′ly Days of Ob-li-ga′tion (ŏb-lĭ-gā′shŭn), days to be kept holy just as Sunday is.

In-ten′tion (ĭn-tĕn′shŭn), reason, purpose.

Ob-serv′ance (ŏb-zûr′văns), keeping holy.

Pro-fane′ (prō-fān′), wicked or irreverent.

Re-quire′ (rē-kwīr′), call for.

Rev′er-ence (rĕv′ĕr-ĕns), great respect.

Ser′vile (sûr′vĭl), performed with bodily labor.

Un-nec′es-sa-ry (ŭn-nĕs′ĕ-sā-rĭ), what we can do without.

345. Q. What is the second Commandment?

A. The second Commandment is: "Thou shalt not take the name of the Lord thy God in vain."

346. Q. What are we commanded by the second Commandment?

A. We are commanded by the second Commandment to speak with reverence of God and of the Saints, and of all holy things, and to keep our lawful oaths and vows.

347. **Q. What is an oath?**
A. An oath is the calling upon God to witness the truth of what we say.

350. **Q. What is a vow?**
A. A vow is a deliberate promise made to God to do something that is pleasing to Him.

351. **Q. Is it a sin not to fulfill our vows?**
A. Not to fulfill our vows is a sin, mortal or venial, according to the nature of the vow and the intention we had in making it.

352. **Q. What is forbidden by the second Commandment?**
A. The second Commandment forbids all false, rash, unjust, and unnecessary oaths, blasphemy, cursing, and profane words.

353. **Q. What is the third Commandment?**
A. The third Commandment is: "Remember thou keep holy the Sabbath day."

355. **Q. How are we to worship God on Sundays and Holy Days of Obligation?**
A. We are to worship God on Sundays and Holy Days of Obligation by hearing Mass, by prayer and by other good works.

358. **Q. What is forbidden by the third Commandment?**
A. The third Commandment forbids all unnecessary servile work and whatever else may hinder the due observance of the Lord's day.

359. **Q. What are servile works?**
A. Servile works are those which require labor rather of body than of mind.

360. Q. Are servile works on Sunday ever lawful?

A. Servile works are lawful on Sunday when the honor of God, the good of our neighbor, or necessity requires them.

LESSON TWENTY-NINTH

From the Fourth to the Seventh Commandment

Bod′i-ly (bŏd′ĭ-lĭ), belonging to the body.
Con-tempt′ (kŏn-tĕmpt′), making little of.
Ha′tred (hā′trĕd), strong dislike.
Mag′is-trates (măj′ĭs-trāts), public officers, like the President, governor, mayor, etc.
Re-venge′ (rē-vĕnj′), desire to pay back an injury.
Seek, look after.
Spir′it-u-al (spĭr′ĭt-ū-ăl), belonging to the soul.
Stub′born-ness (stŭb′ẽrn-nĕs), wanting to have our own way.
Su-pe′ri-ors (sū-pē′rĭ-ẽrz), those placed over us.
Un′ion (ūn′yŭn), as one.
Wel′fare (wĕl′fâr), good fortune.

361. Q. What is the fourth Commandment?
A. The fourth Commandment is: "Honor thy father and thy mother."

362. Q. What are we commanded by the fourth Commandment?
A. We are commanded by the fourth Commandment to honor, love, and obey our parents in all that is not sin.

363. Q. Are we bound to honor and obey others than our parents?
A. We are also bound to honor and obey our bishops, pastors, magistrates, teachers, and other lawful superiors.

365. **Q. What is forbidden by the fourth Commandment?**
A. The fourth Commandment forbids all disobedience, contempt, and stubbornness towards our parents or lawful superiors.

366. **Q. What is the fifth Commandment?**
A. The fifth Commandment is: "Thou shalt not kill."

367. **Q. What are we commanded by the fifth Commandment?**
A. We are commanded by the fifth Commandment to live in peace and union with our neighbor, to respect his rights, to seek his spiritual and bodily welfare, and to take proper care of our own life and health.

368. **Q. What is forbidden by the fifth Commandment?**
A. The fifth Commandment forbids all willful murder, fighting, anger, hatred, revenge, and bad example.

369. **Q. What is the sixth Commandment?**
A. The sixth Commandment is: "Thou shalt not commit adultery."

370. **Q. What are we commanded by the sixth Commandment?**
A. We are commanded by the sixth Commandment to be pure in thought and modest in all our looks, words and actions.

371. **Q. What is forbidden by the sixth Commandment?**
A. The sixth Commandment forbids all unchaste freedom with another's wife or husband; also all immodesty with ourselves or others in looks, dress, words or actions.

372. Q. Does the sixth Commandment forbid the reading of bad and immodest books and newspapers?

A. The sixth Commandment does forbid the reading of bad and immodest books and newspapers.

LESSON THIRTIETH

From the Seventh to the End of the Tenth Commandment

Back′bit′ing (băk′bīt′ĭng), talking evil of one who is absent.

Ill′-got′ten (ĭl′gŏt′ĕn), gotten unjustly.

Rash judg′ments (răsh jŭj′mĕnts), thinking or saying things about another of which we are not sure.

Re-pair′ (rē-pâr′) **the dam′age** (dăm′ȧj), make good the harm done.

Rep′u-ta′tion (rĕp′ū-tā′shŭn), good name.

Re-spect′ (rē-spĕkt′) **their prop′-er-ty** (prŏp′ĕr-tĭ), not to take or spoil anything that belongs to another.

Slan′ders (slăn′dẽrz), wicked lies about another.

Un-just′ (ŭn-jŭst′), that which is against the rights of another.

373. Q. What is the seventh Commandment?

A. The seventh Commandment is: "Thou shalt not steal."

374. Q. What are we commanded by the seventh Commandment?

A. By the seventh Commandment we are commanded to give to all men what belongs to them and to respect their property.

375. Q. What is forbidden by the seventh Commandment?

A. The seventh Commandment forbids all unjust taking or keeping what belongs to another.

376. **Q. Are we bound to restore ill-gotten goods?**
A. We are bound to restore ill-gotten goods, or the value of them, as far as we are able; otherwise we cannot be forgiven.

377. **Q. Are we obliged to repair the damage we have unjustly caused?**
A. We are bound to repair the damage we have unjustly caused.

378. **Q. What is the eighth Commandment?**
A. The eighth Commandment is: "Thou shalt not bear false witness against thy neighbor."

379. **Q. What are we commanded by the eighth Commandment?**
A. We are commanded by the eighth Commandment to speak the truth in all things, and to be careful of the honor and reputation of every one.

380. **Q. What is forbidden by the eighth Commandment?**
A. The eighth Commandment forbids all rash judgments, backbiting, slanders, and lies.

382. **Q. What is the ninth Commandment?**
A. The ninth Commandment is: "Thou shalt not covet thy neighbor's wife."

383. **Q. What are we commanded by the ninth Commandment?**
A. We are commanded by the ninth Commandment to keep ourselves pure in thought and desire.

384. Q. What is forbidden by the ninth Commandment?

A. The ninth Commandment forbids unchaste thoughts, desires of another's wife or husband, and all other unlawful impure thoughts and desires.

386. Q. What is the tenth Commandment?

A. The tenth Commandment is: "Thou shalt not covet thy neighbor's goods."

387. Q. What are we commanded by the tenth Commandment?

A. By the tenth Commandment we are commanded to be content with what we have, and to rejoice in our neighbor's welfare.

388. Q. What is forbidden by the tenth Commandment?

A. The tenth Commandment forbids all desires to take or keep wrongfully what belongs to another.

LESSON THIRTY-FIRST

On the First and Second Commandments of the Church

Ab-stain′ (ăb-stān′), not to eat meat.

Ab′sti-nence (ăb′stĭ-nĕns), doing without meat.

Charge (chärj), care.

Con-trib′ute (kŏn-trĭb′ūt), to pay our share.

Fast (fȧst), to eat only one full meal in the day.

Flesh-meat, animal food of all kinds, except fish.

Kin′dred (kĭn′drĕd), blood relationship.

Mor′ti-fy (môr′tĭ-fī), to deaden, keep down.

Se′ri-ous rea′son (sē′rĭ-ŭs rē′z'n), a very good reason.

Sol′em-nize (sŏl′ĕm-nīz), to have the wedding blessing and great display.

Third degree, second cousins.

389. Q. Which are the chief commandments of the Church?

A. The chief commandments of the Church are six:

1. To hear Mass on Sundays and Holy Days of Obligation.
2. To fast and abstain on the days appointed.
3. To confess at least once a year.
4. To receive the Holy Eucharist during the Easter time.
5. To contribute to the support of our pastors.

6. Not to marry persons who are not Catholics, or who are related to us within the third degree of kindred, nor privately without witnesses, nor to solemnize marriage at forbidden times.

390. Q. Is it a mortal sin not to hear Mass on a Sunday or a Holy Day of Obligation?

A. It is a mortal sin not to hear Mass on a Sunday or Holy Day of Obligation unless we are excused for a serious reason. They also commit a mortal sin who, having others under their charge, hinder them from hearing Mass, without a sufficient reason.

393. Q. What do you mean by fast-days?

A. By fast-days I mean days on which we are allowed but one full meal.

394. Q. What do you mean by days of abstinence?

A. By days of abstinence, I mean days on which we are forbidden to eat flesh-meat, but are allowed the usual number of meals.

395. Q. Why does the Church command us to fast and abstain?

A. The Church commands us to fast and abstain in order that we may mortify our passions and satisfy for our sins.

LESSON THIRTY-SECOND

On the Third, Fourth, Fifth, and Sixth Commandments of the Church

Neg-lects′ (nĕg-lĕkts′), omits, fails to attend to.

O-bliged′ (ō-blījd′), bound.

Under pain of mortal sin, guilty of mortal sin if we disobey.

397. Q. What is meant by the command of confessing at least once a year?

A. By the command of confessing at least once a year is meant that we are obliged, under pain of mortal sin, to go to Confession within the year.

400. Q. What sin does he commit who neglects to receive Communion during the Easter time?

A. He who neglects to receive Communion during the Easter time commits a mortal sin.

401. Q. What is the Easter time?

A. The Easter time is, in this country, the time between the first Sunday of Lent and Trinity Sunday.

402. Q. Are we obliged to contribute to the support of our pastors?

A. We are obliged to contribute to the support of our pastors, and to bear our share in the expenses of the Church and school.

LESSON THIRTY-THIRD

On the Last Judgment and the Resurrection, Hell, Purgatory and Heaven

Con-demned′ (kŏn-dĕmd′), sentenced.

De-prived′ (dē-prīvd′), kept from.

Dread′ful (drĕd′fŭl), apt to make us afraid.

E-ter′nal (ē-tĕr′năl), never ending.

E-ter′ni-ty (ē-tĕr′nĭ-tĭ), for ever and ever.

Gen′er-al (jĕn′ĕr-ăl), belonging to all.

Im-me′di-ate-ly (ĭ-mē′dĭ-ȧt-lĭ), at once.

Judge, to reward or punish.

Par-tic′u-lar (pär-tĭk′ū-lȧr), belonging to one only.

State, a mode of being, a kind of life.

Tor′ments (tôr′mĕnts), pains, sufferings.

Un′der-go′ (ŭn′dĕr-gō′), to stand or bear.

U-nit′ed (ū-nīt′ĕd), joined.

408. Q. When will Christ judge us?

A. Christ will judge us immediately after our death, and on the last day.

409. Q. What is the judgment called which we have to undergo immediately after death?

A. The judgment we have to undergo immediately after death is called the Particular Judgment.

410. Q. What is the judgment called which all men have to undergo on the last day?

A. The judgment which all men have to undergo on the last day is called the General Judgment.

412. Q. What are the rewards or punishments appointed for men's souls after the Particular Judgment?

A. The rewards or punishments appointed for men's souls after the Particular Judgment are Heaven, Purgatory and Hell.

413. Q. What is Hell?

A. Hell is a state to which the wicked are condemned, and in which they are deprived of the sight of God for all eternity, and are in dreadful torments.

414. Q. What is Purgatory?

A. Purgatory is the state in which those suffer for a time who die guilty of venial sins, or without having satisfied for the punishment due to their sins.

417. Q. Will our bodies share in the reward or punishment of our souls?

A. Our bodies will share in the reward or punishment of our souls, because through the resurrection they will again be united to them.

420. Q. What is Heaven?

A. Heaven is the state of everlasting life in which we see God face to face, are made like unto Him in glory, and enjoy eternal happiness.

MORNING PRAYERS

As soon as you awake, think of God. Make the Sign of the Cross and say:

✠ In the name of the Father, and of the Son, and of the Holy Ghost. Amen.

Then dress quickly and kneel down. Now say the *Our Father*, the *Hail Mary*, the *Apostles' Creed*, the *Confiteor* and the *Acts of Faith*, *Hope*, *Love* and *Contrition* which you have probably memorized. If you do not know them by heart you will find them on pages 1-5.

Then if you have time also say the following prayers:

To the Blessed Virgin

My Lady, and my Mother, remember I am thine; protect and defend me as thy property and possession.

To St. Joseph

Saint Joseph, model and patron of those who love the Sacred Heart of Jesus, pray for us.

To the Guardian Angel

Angel of God, my guardian dear,
To whom His love commits me here,
Ever this day be at my side,
To light and guard, to rule and guide. Amen.
God bless Papa and Mamma. God bless brothers and sisters, and all my friends. God bless me, and make me a good child.

For the Faithful Departed

Eternal rest give unto them, O Lord. And let perpetual light shine upon them. May they rest in peace. Amen.

Glory be to the Father, and to the Son, and to the Holy Ghost. As it was in the beginning, is now, and ever shall be, world without end. Amen.

Make the Sign of the Cross.

EVENING PRAYERS

Never go to bed without thanking God for all the benefits you have received during the day and during your whole life. Kneel down. Make the Sign of the Cross. Then say the *Our Father*, *Hail Mary*, the *Apostles' Creed*, the *Confiteor*, and *Glory Be*.

Now think how you have acted during the day. Are there any big sins on your soul? Any little sins? Try to tell Jesus how sorry you are for all your sins, and say the *Act of Contrition* (p. 4).

Jesus, Mary, Joseph, I give you my heart and my soul.
Jesus, Mary, Joseph, assist me in my last agony.
Jesus, Mary, Joseph, may I breathe forth my soul in peace with you.
O my God, bless my father, mother, and all my relatives and friends.
May the souls of the faithful departed, through the mercy of God, rest in peace. Amen.

Bless yourself with holy water.

✠ In the name of the Father, and of the Son, and of the Holy Ghost. Amen.

PRAYERS FOR MASS[1]

Remember that the church is the house of God, where the living God dwells. And where God is, His holy angels too are present. In church, therefore, be reverent and modest in your behavior, and always be on time. When you enter, bless yourself with holy water and go quietly to your seat, genuflect on your right knee and enter the pew.

Prayer before Mass

> O my God, I am only a child; help me to be attentive, and to pray with all my heart during this holy Mass.

The priest comes out to begin Mass.

Stand.

---

1. The Mass prayers are an arrangement of those contained in Father Finn's *Prayer Book for Catholic Youth* (also known as Father Finn's *Boys' and Girls' Prayer Book*). They follow closely in simplified language the spirit and liturgy of the "Ordinary of the Mass," so that children will become readily accustomed to using the Church's own prayers and follow the priest at the altar. The rubrics when to sit, stand, or kneel at Low Mass are given.

   If it is found desirable to have the children recite prayers aloud and in unison at Mass, certain parts suitable for this purpose are marked with an asterisk (*).

The priest carries in his hands the chalice, covered with a cloth. The priest goes up to the middle of the altar, and sets down the chalice. Then he goes to the right side and opens the book.

After that he comes down to the foot of the altar, and makes the Sign of the Cross.

The Mass of the Catechumens

(***From the Beginning to the Offertory***)

Kneel.

*In the name of the Father, and of the Son, and of the Holy Ghost. Amen.

*I will go in to the altar of God, to God Who gives joy to my youth.

*Judge me, O God. Keep me safe from all evil.

Glory be to the Father, and to the Son and to the Holy Ghost.

As it was in the beginning, is now and ever shall be, world without end. Amen.

I will go in to the altar of God,
To God Who gives joy to my youth.

Here the priest makes the Sign of the Cross.

Our help is in the name of the Lord.
Who made Heaven and earth.

The priest, bowing down, says the *Confiteor*. Then the altar-boys bow and say it after him. Read it as on p. 2.

The priest goes up to the altar and says:

O Lord, we beg You, by the goodness of Your Saints whose relics are here, and of all Your Saints, to forgive us all our sins.

The Introit and Kyrie Eleison

The priest goes to the right side of the altar and reads from the book. Then going back to the middle of the altar he says the *Kyrie Eleison*.

The Gloria

Glory be to God on high, and on earth peace to men of good will. We praise You. We bless You. We glorify You. We give You thanks for Your great glory, O Lord God, heavenly King, God the Father almighty. O Lord God, Son of the Father, Who take away the sins of the world, have mercy on us. You only, O Jesus Christ, with the Holy Ghost, are most high in the Glory of God the Father. Amen.

The priest turns to the people and says:

The Lord be with you.
And with your spirit.

The Collect

The priest goes to the right side of the altar and reads from the book.

> *Let us pray: *Let Your grace and pity guide our hearts, we beg You, O Lord. For without You we cannot please You. Through Our Lord, Jesus Christ, Your Son, Who lives and reigns with You in the unity of the Holy Ghost, world without end. Amen.

The Epistle

The Epistle is a letter. Most of these letters were written by St. Paul. The priest now reads one of these. You may read the following:

> Dear children: Be happy, be good, be brave; agree with one another, and be at peace. The grace of Our Lord Jesus Christ, God's love, and the wisdom of the Holy Ghost be with you all. Amen.
>
> Thanks be to God.

The altar-boy carries the book to the left side of the altar. The priest bows at the middle of the altar and says a prayer.

The Gospel

The priest goes to the left and reads from the book.

Stand.

While Jesus was speaking to the people, mothers brought their children to Him, that He might bless them. The disciples told them not to bother Jesus. But Jesus said, "Suffer the little children to come to Me and forbid them not. For of such is the kingdom of Heaven." And Jesus blessed the children.

Praise be to You, O Christ.

Sit.

The priest now turns back to the middle of the altar and says the *Creed*. You also say it (see p. 1).

The Mass of the Faithful

(From the Offertory to the Communion)

The Offering of the Host

The priest takes the cloth off the chalice. Then he holds up a small gold plate on which is the bread, called the *host*.

*Take, O holy Father, almighty and eternal God, this spotless host which I, Your unworthy servant, offer to You for my many sins and for all who serve You, living and dead. May it help them and me to gain eternal life.

The priest goes to the right side of the altar. He pours wine and water into the chalice. Then the priest goes back to the middle of the altar and raises the chalice.

The Offering of the Chalice

*We offer You, O Lord, this chalice. May it help us and all the world to gain eternal life. Amen.

The priest goes to the right side of the altar to wash his hands.

Returning to the middle of the altar, the priest bows down and says some prayers. Then he turns to the people and says the *Orate Fratres.*

Now the priest prays in a low voice and then in a louder voice he says the Preface:

> Truly, it is right and just that we should at all times and in all places give thanks to You, O holy Lord, Father almighty, Who, with Your only Son and the Holy Ghost are one God, one Lord. All the angels daily praise You, singing with one voice:

**The Sanctus*

> Holy, holy, holy Lord, God of hosts.
> Heaven and earth are full of Your glory.
> Hosanna in the highest.

The bell is rung three times.

Kneel.

THE CANON[2]

The priest bows low and kisses the altar.

> O most merciful Father, we pray You, through Jesus Christ, Your Son, Our Lord, to take and bless these gifts. We offer them to You for Your holy Catholic Church, for our Pope and Bishop and for all those in the Catholic Faith.

Prayer for the Living

Be mindful, O Lord, of Your servants (*name those for whom you wish to pray especially*), and all who are now hearing this Mass. Hear, O Lord, the prayers they are offering for themselves, their friends and their families.

The Consecration of the Host

The priest now bends low over the host and says:

THIS IS MY BODY.

At these words, the bread is changed into the Body of Our Lord. The bell rings. The priest kneels and then raises the Sacred Body of Our Lord. Now look at the Sacred Host and say: "My Lord and my God." Then bow your head as the priest kneels again.

The Consecration of the Wine

The priest bends over the chalice and says:

THIS IS THE CHALICE OF MY BLOOD.

At these words, the wine becomes the Precious Blood of Our Lord. The bell rings. The priest kneels and then raises the Chalice. Now the priest continues to pray silently. Look at the Chalice and say: "Jesus in the Blessed Sacrament, have mercy on us."

The priest kneels. The bell rings again. The priest prays silently.

2. By a Decree of the Church (August 4, 1922), the prayers during the Canon, i.e., from the *Sanctus* to the *Pater Noster*, must be said in silence.

Prayer for the Dead

> Remember also, O Lord, Your servants (*here name dead relatives and friends*) who have gone before us with the sign of faith and sleep the sleep of peace.

Now the priest says the *Pater Noster*. Say the *Our Father*. Soon after the priest strikes his breast and says the *Agnus Dei*.

The Priest's Communion

The priest after saying some prayers silently, takes the Sacred Host and paten in his left hand and striking his breast with the right hand says (the bell rings three times):

> *O Lord, I am not worthy that You should enter under my roof. Say but the word and my soul shall be healed.

The priest bows down and receives the Body of Our Lord. He remains in prayer for a short time. Then he uncovers the chalice and drinks the Sacred Blood of Our Lord.

The Communion of the People

The priest now opens the tabernacle and takes out the Blessed Sacrament to give Holy Communion to the people. Turning to the people and holding the ciborium in his left hand, he lifts up a Sacred Host to the people in his right hand. Now say with the priest three times:

> "Lord, I am not worthy that You should enter my soul; say but the word and my soul shall be healed."

After the Communion

Having replaced the Blessed Sacrament in the tabernacle, the priest after taking water and wine, covers the chalice and goes to the right side of the altar to read from the book. Then going back to the middle he turns to the people and says:

> The Lord be with you.
> And with your spirit.

Then the priest again goes to the right side of the altar and reads:

The Prayers after Communion

> *Let us pray: We have been filled with Your gifts, O Lord. Grant that they may make us clean and strong. May the gift of this divine Sacrament keep us pure, O Lord. Through the help of the Blessed Virgin, of St. Joseph, of Sts. Peter and Paul and all the Saints, may it free us from all evil.

The priest goes back to the middle of the altar and turning to the people says:

> The Lord be with you.
> And with your spirit.
> Go, the Mass is ended.
> Thanks be to God.

The Blessing

The priest bows down and says a prayer. Then turning to the people he blesses them saying:

> May almighty God, the Father, Son, and Holy Ghost, bless you. Amen.

The priest goes to the left side of the altar.

Stand.

> The Lord be with you.
> And with your spirit.

The Last Gospel

The priest makes a cross on forehead, lips, and breast, and says the Gospel of St. John.

Remain standing until the priest has left the sanctuary or kneels down to say the prayers after Mass.

THE RIGHT MANNER OF CONFESSING[1]

Prayer before Examining Your Conscience

O Holy Spirit, help me to know all my sins. Help me to remember that Jesus died for me. Help me to make a good Confession and I promise that I will try never to sin again.

Now think of your sins.

Prayer before Entering the Confessional

O God, I am very sorry for all my sins. I promise that I will try to be good and never again to hurt You by sin. Dear Jesus, help me. Mother of God, pray that I may please Your Son by true sorrow for my sins.

1. From Father Finn's *Prayer Book for Catholic Youth.*

When your turn comes, go into the confession box. Make the Sign of the Cross and wait till the priest opens the little door. Say what you have been taught to say. Or you may say this:

> Bless me, Father, for I have sinned. It is (*say how long*) since my last Confession. Since then I have committed these sins.

Now tell all your sins and how many times you committed each. If there is something you don't know how to tell, just say, "Please help me, Father," and the priest will help you. After you have told all your sins, say what you have been taught to say. Or you may say:

> That is all, Father.

In case you have no big sins to confess, it is well to end your Confession with: "In my past life I sinned through anger or impurity" (or some sin that you know you did and that you are sorry for). The priest tells you what prayers to say for a penance. Then he tells you to say the *Act of Contrition*. When you come out, kneel down near the altar. Say your penance at once. Then thank God for being so good to you.

COMMUNION PRAYERS

Acts before Communion

Act of Faith

Jesus Christ, my Sovereign Lord, I firmly believe that Thou art really present in the Holy Eucharist, and that it is Thy body, Thy blood, Thy soul, and Thy divinity that I shall receive in that Adorable Sacrament.

Act of Hope

Thou hast said, O my God, that those hoping in Thee shall never be confounded. I place all my confidence in Thy promises, and I hope that, having nourished myself with Thy body on earth, I shall have the happiness of seeing and possessing Thee eternally in Heaven.

Act of Love

O my divine Jesus, Who hast so loved me as to nourish me with Thy adorable flesh, I love Thee with all my heart and above all things; I wish to live and die in Thy holy love.

Act of Humility

My Saviour and my God, Thou art all sanctity. I am not worthy that Thou shouldst enter my heart; yet, speak but the word and my soul shall be healed.

Act of Desire

My soul desires Thee, O my God! Thou art its joy and happiness. Come, O divine Jesus, come into my heart; it desires ardently to receive Thee.

ACTS AFTER COMMUNION

Act of Adoration

I adore Thee, O Jesus, as the Lamb of God immolated for the salvation of mankind. I join in the profound adoration which the angels and Saints pay to Thee in Heaven.

Act of Thanksgiving

Lord, Thou hast looked on my unworthiness. I was sick, and Thou hast healed me. I was poor, and Thou hast bestowed upon me Thy numberless benefits. How shall I be able to thank Thee, O my Lord, for all Thy favors? I will invoke Thy holy Name, and eternally sing Thy mercies.

Act of Offering

What can I offer Thee, O my God, for the grace of having given Thyself to me? I consecrate to Thy glory my body, my soul, and all that I possess! Dispose of me according to Thy holy Will.

Act of Petition

My divine Redeemer, Thou hast taken possession of me. Do not let the enemy of my salvation ravish the precious treasure I bear in my heart. Preserve me from all sin, and defend me against temptation, that I may persevere until death in the practice of Thy holy law. Amen.

THE ROSARY OF THE BLESSED VIRGIN

The Five Joyful Mysteries

(Assigned for Mondays and Thursdays throughout the year, the Sundays of Advent and after Epiphany until Lent.)

First Mystery. The Annunciation.
Second Mystery. The Visitation.
Third Mystery. The Nativity.
Fourth Mystery. The Presentation.
Fifth Mystery. The Finding of the Child Jesus in the Temple.

The Five Sorrowful Mysteries

(For Tuesdays and Fridays throughout the year and Sundays in Lent.)

First Mystery. The Prayer and Bloody Sweat of our blessed Saviour in the Garden.
Second Mystery. The Scourging of Jesus at the Pillar.
Third Mystery. The Crowning of Jesus with Thorns.
Fourth Mystery. Jesus Carrying His Cross.
Fifth Mystery. The Crucifixion.

The Five Glorious Mysteries

(For Wednesdays and Saturdays throughout the year and Sundays after Easter until after Advent.)

First Mystery. The Resurrection.
Second Mystery. The Ascension.
Third Mystery. The Descent of the Holy Ghost.
Fourth Mystery. The Assumption.
Fifth Mystery. The Crowning of the Blessed Virgin.

THE STATIONS OF THE CROSS

A plenary indulgence can be gained each time one makes the Stations, subject to the usual conditions.

To make the Stations and gain the indulgences, no special prayer is required. We have but to begin at the first Station and go around to the last, thinking devoutly of the Passion and death of Christ

HYMNS

Come, Holy Ghost, Creator Blest

1. Come, Holy Ghost, Creator blest,
And in our hearts take up Thy rest;
Come with Thy grace and heavenly aid
To fill the hearts which Thou hast made.

2. O Comforter, to Thee we cry,
Thou heavenly Gift of God most high,
Thou Fount of life and Fire of love,
And sweet Anointing from above.

3. Praise we the Father and the Son,
And Holy Spirit with them One;
And may the Son on us bestow
The gifts that from the Spirit flow.

O Salutaris

1. O Salutaris Hostia!
   Quae coeli pandis ostium:
   Bella premunt hostilia,
   Da robur, fer auxilium.

2. Uni trinoque Domino
   Sit sempiterna gloria,
   Qui vitam sine termino
   Nobis donet in Patria.
   Amen.

Tantum Ergo

1. Tantum ergo Sacramentum
   Veneremur cernui;
   Et antiquum documentum
   Novo cedat ritui;
   Praestet fides supplementum
   Sensuum defectui.

2. Genitori, Genitoque
   Laus et jubilatio,
   Salus, honor, virtus quoque
   Sit et benedictio;
   Procedenti ab utroque
   Compar sit laudatio.
   Amen.

V. Panem de coelo praestitisti eis.
R. Omne delectamentum in se habentem.

Adeste Fideles

1. Adeste, fideles,
Laeti triumphantes;
Venite, venite in Bethlehem;
Natum videte
Regem Angelorum,
Venite, adoremus,
Venite, adoremus,
Venite, adoremus Dominum.

2. Deum de Deo,
Lumen de lumine,
Gestant puellae viscera;
Deum verum,
Genitum non factum,
Venite, etc.

3. Cantet nunc Io!
Chorus Angelorum;
Cantet nunc aula coelestium.
Gloria
In excelsis Deo,
Venite, etc.

4. Ergo, qui natus
Die hodierna,
Jesu! tibi sit gloria,
Patris aeterni
Verbum caro factum,
Venite, etc.

Jesus, My Lord, My God

(Rev. F. W. Faber)

1. Jesus, my Lord, my God, my all!
   How can I love Thee as I ought?
And how revere this wondrous gift,
   So far surpassing hope or thought?

Chorus Sweet Sacrament! We Thee adore,
Oh, make us love Thee more and more,
Oh, make us love Thee more and more.

2. Had I but Mary's sinless heart
   To love Thee with, my dearest King,
Oh, with what bursts of fervent praise
   Thy goodness, Jesus, would I sing!

To Jesus' Heart All Burning

(Rev. A. J. Christie, S.J.)

1. To Jesus' Heart, all burning
   With fervent love for men,
My heart with fondest yearning
   Shall raise the joyful strain.

Chorus While ages course along,
Blest be with loudest song
The Sacred Heart of Jesus
By every heart and tongue.

2. O Heart for me on fire
   With love no man can speak,
My yet untold desire
   God gives me for Thy sake.

3. Too true I have forsaken
   Thy flock by wilful sin;
Yet now let me be taken
   Back to Thy fold again.

Jesus, Gentlest Saviour

(Rev. F. W. Faber)

1. Jesus, gentlest Saviour!
   God of might and power;
Thou Thyself art dwelling
   In us at this hour.
Nature cannot hold Thee,
   Heav'n is all too strait
For Thine endless glory,
   And Thy royal state.

2. Out beyond the shining
   Of the farthest star,
Thou art ever stretching
   Infinitely far.
Yet the hearts of children
   Hold what worlds cannot,
And the God of wonders
   Loves the lowly spot.

Jesus! Saviour of My Soul

1. Jesus! Saviour of my soul,
   Let me to Thy refuge fly,
   While the nearer waters roll,
   While the tempest still is nigh.

Chorus Hide me, O my Saviour, hide
   Till the storm of life is past;
   Safe into Thy haven guide,
   O receive my soul at last.
   Jesus! Saviour of my soul,
   Let me to Thy refuge fly;
   Ave, Ave, Jesus mild,
   Deign to hear Thy lowly child.

2. Other refuge have I none,
   Hangs my helpless soul on Thee,
   Leave, oh, leave me not alone,
   Still support and strengthen me.

Jesus, the Very Thought of Thee

(Rev. E. Caswall)

1. Jesus, the very thought of Thee
   With rapture fills my breast;
   But sweeter far Thy Face to see,
   And in Thy presence rest.

2. Nor voice can sing, nor heart can frame,
   Nor can the mem'ry find
   A sweeter sound than Thy blest Name,
   O Saviour of mankind!

3. Jesus, our only joy be Thou,
   As Thou our prize wilt be;
   O Jesus, be our glory now
   And through eternity.

What Happiness Can Equal Mine?

(Rev. F. W. Faber)

1. What happiness can equal mine?
   I've found the object of my love:
   My Jesus dear, my King Divine,
   Is come to me from heav'n above;
   He chose my heart for His abode,
   He there becomes my daily bread;
   There on me flows His healing blood;
   There with His flesh my soul is fed.

Chorus What happiness can equal mine?
I've found the object of my love:
My Jesus dear, my King Divine,
Is come to me from heav'n above.

2. I am my love's, and He is mine:
In me He dwells, in Him I live;
What greater treasures could I find?
And could, ye heavens, a greater give?
O sacred banquet, heav'nly feast!
O overflowing source of grace,
Where God the food, and man, the guest,
Meet and unite in sweet embrace!

The Love of Jesus

1. O the priceless love of Jesus:
O the strength of grace divine;
All His gifts are showered upon me,
All His blessings may be mine.
He is throned in Heavenly glory
Where no sin nor death can be;
Yet He loves me in this darkness,
Yet He does not turn from me.

2. I am blind, and poor, and wretched,
   By temptations sorely tried;
Yet His watchful care abounding
   Keeps me ever at His side.
He is God and King Eternal,
   Higher than all height can be;
Yet His Heart is with me always,
   Yet He stoopeth down to me.

Holy God, We Praise Thy Name

(Rev. C. Walworth)

1. Holy God, we praise Thy name,
   Lord of all, we bow before Thee!
All on earth Thy sceptre claim,
   All in heav'n above adore Thee.
Infinite Thy vast domain,
   Everlasting is Thy name.

2. Hark! the loud celestial hymn,
   Angel choirs above are raising!
Cherubim and Seraphim,
   In unceasing chorus praising.
Fill the heavens with sweet accord;
   Holy! Holy! Holy Lord.

Hail, Heavenly Queen!

1. Hail, heavenly Queen! Hail, foamy ocean star!
   O be our guide, diffuse thy beams afar;
   Hail, Mother of God! above all virgins blest,
   Hail, happy gate of heav'n's eternal rest.

Chorus Hail foamy ocean star! Hail, heav'nly Queen!
   O be our guide to endless joys unseen.

2. "Hail, full of grace," with Gabriel we repeat;
   Thee, Queen of heav'n, from him we learn to greet;
   Then give us peace which heav'n alone can give,
   And dead thro' Eve, thro' Mary let us live.

Mother Dear, Oh, Pray for Me

1. Mother dear, oh, pray for me,
   Whilst far from heav'n and thee
   I wander in a fragile bark,
   O'er life's tempestuous sea;
   O Virgin Mother, from thy throne,
   So bright in bliss above,
   Protect thy child and cheer my path,
   With thy sweet smile of love.

Chorus Mother dear, remember me,
   And never cease thy care,
   Till in Heaven eternally
   Thy love and bliss I share.

2. Mother dear, oh, pray for me,
   Should pleasure's siren lay
   E'er tempt thy child to wander far
   From virtue's path away;
   When thorns beset life's devious way,
   And darkling waters flow,
   Then, Mary, aid thy weeping child,
   Thyself a mother show.

Ora Pro Me

1. Ave Maria! bright and pure,
   Hear, O hear me when I pray,
   Pains and pleasures try the pilgrim
   On his long and dreary way.
   Fears and perils are around me,
   Ave Maria! bright and pure,
   Ora pro me, ora pro me.

2. Ave Maria! Queen of Heaven,
   Teach, O teach me to obey,
   Lead me on, tho' fierce temptations
   Stand and meet me in the way.
   When I fail and faint, my Mother,
   Ave Maria! bright and pure,
   Ora pro me, ora pro me.

I'll Sing a Hymn to Mary

(Rev. Fr. Wyse)

I'll sing a hymn to Mary,
The Mother of my God,
The Virgin of all Virgins,
Of David's royal blood.
Oh, teach me, holy Mary
A loving song to frame,
When wicked men blaspheme thee
To love and bless thy name.

When troubles dark afflict me
In sorrow and in care,
Thy light doth ever guide me
O beauteous Morning Star.
Lo, I'll be ever ready
Thy goodly help to claim,
When wicked men blaspheme thee
I'll love and bless thy name.

Daily, Daily Sing to Mary

1. Daily, daily sing to Mary
Sing, my soul, her praises due;
All her feasts, her actions worship,
With the heart's devotion true.
Lost in wond'ring contemplation,
Be her majesty confess'd;
Call her Mother, call her Virgin,
Happy Mother, Virgin blest.

2. She is mighty to deliver;
   Call her, trust her lovingly;
When the tempest rages round thee,
   She will calm the troubled sea.
Gifts of Heaven she has given,
   Noble Lady, to our race;
She the Queen who decks her subject,
   With the light of God's own grace.

Hymn to St. Joseph

1. With grateful hearts we breathe today
   The tender accents of our love.
We carol forth a little lay
   To thee, great Saint in Heaven above.

Chorus O Joseph dear, from thy bright throne,
   Incline thine ear unto our prayer.
And o'er us all as o'er thine own,
   Extend thy fond paternal care,
And o'er us all as o'er thine own,
Extend thy fond paternal care,
Extend thy fond paternal care.

2. More favored than earth's greatest king.
   Thou wert the guardian of that Child,
Around whose crib full choirs did sing,
   With cadenced voices soft and mild.

Dear Guardian of Mary

(Rev. F. W. Faber)

1. Dear Guardian of Mary! dear nurse of her child!
Life's ways are full weary, the desert is wild;
Bleak sands are all round us, no home can we see;
Sweet Spouse of Our Lady! we lean upon thee.
2. For thou to the pilgrim art father and guide,
And Jesus and Mary felt safe at thy side;
Ah! blessed Saint Joseph, how safe should I be,
Sweet Spouse of Our Lady! if thou wert with me.

Dear Angel, Ever at My Side

(Rev. F. W. Faber)

1. Dear Angel, ever at my side,
   How loving must thou be,
To leave thy home in Heaven to guide
   A little child like me.

2. Thy beautiful and shining face
   I see not, though so near;
The sweetness of thy soft, low voice
   I am too deaf to hear.

Hymn at the Communion

O Lord, I am not worthy
  That Thou shouldst come to me,
But speak the words of comfort,
  My spirit healed shall be.

And humbly I'll receive Thee,
  The bridegroom of my soul,
No more by sin to grieve Thee,
  Or fly Thy sweet control.